Adventures with Spirit

Adventures with Spirit

The Healing Journey

Sue Ostapowich

Copyright © 2012 by Sue Ostapowich.

Library of Congress Control Number: 2011911395
ISBN: Hardcover   978-1-4628-4631-3
               Softcover   978-1-4628-4630-6
               Ebook   978-1-4628-4632-0

This book was printed in the United States of America.

To order additional copies of this book, contact:
Xlibris Corporation
1-888-795-4274
www.Xlibris.com
Orders@Xlibris.com
89835

CONTENTS

This book is dedicated to my dear Mother who suffered in silence,

and to all others who suffer in silence,

and to those who don't, as yet, know their pain,

and to those who cause the suffering.

"Faith makes things possible — not easy" (anonymous, 2000)

Acknowledgements and heartfelt gratitude to:

- ❖ all those around me in the 'office' at the time of my 'awakening', for putting up with me and supporting me during the trying times and during the joyful times, especially Linda, Lynn, Glady, Heather, Jim, Dave, and Betty.

- ❖ my Demon Slayer, who must have thought—at least on occasion, "who or what is this crazy lady?"

- ❖ my children, who have always supported me.

- ❖ my friend Lucille, who kept me from flying too high into the sky!

- ❖ the book Writing Spirit — by Lynn V. Andrews, which gave me inspiration and courage to put down the story which wanted to be written.

- ❖ my friend and editor Anna Olson, who pushed and pulled me—with some success—to be grammatically correct.

- ❖ my sister Mary, who has supported me faithfully during my journey and listened even when I'm sure she was tired of listening!

- ❖ my mother's Spirit, which kept whispering in my ear to "get it done!"

- ❖ the 'Great Spirit', that continued to push me in so many ways, keeping me to my promises and providing me with the supports and resources I needed to manifest this work.

- ❖ all my 'Spirit guides'—named or unnamed—I will always value your wise counsel.

"One small afterthought . . . There is a tiny little bud on the end
of a branch on a tree in
the middle of the garden; be still and know; the most exquisite
blossom that ever was stands ready to open and flower.
Open your eyes to see: She blooms with time. She blooms with
love. Life is sacred
and just as life guards you, you are life's blessed guardian."

Priestess – Woman as Sacred Celebrant
Pamela Eakins – 1996

INTRODUCTION

THIS IS THE true story of how Spirit found me, offering me a
new way of being, bringing new meaning and purpose to my
existence; a story which may serve to inspire and open new doors for
you. Life had become empty and meaningless for me after the painful
break-up of a long, difficult marriage. I did not really care whether I
lived or died. Life was simply a routine; joyless and empty.

But something inside of me said it was not yet over, that there was
more and it was up to me to push forward.

And push I did. Spirit must have been waiting for its opportunity as
I could not have come up with a better plan of self-help—and certainly,
I could not have found a better counsellor to support me in my journey
of emotional and mental healing.

In this first of three books in a series titled "Adventures With
Spirit" I tell the story of the first few months of my new life during
which Spirit led me down a path of life changing experiences, offering
me moments of personal healing and revelations and insights about
life itself which, I came to understand, I was to share with others.
These healing moments and revelations were reflected in a series of
poems—spontaneously written at the time—short and focused on the

thought, feeling or revelation of that moment, and are included in the chapters of this book which best reflect their content.

I believe these messages came directly from Spirit, from God. Some people with whom I shared my belief at the time disputed this, suggesting that what was happening was a normal experience for someone after having gone through such emotional trauma and changes in life. I did not agree and repeatedly told others that "No, this was being gifted to me from someplace outside of my own mind." And that "I felt like a conduit" and did not feel personally responsible for my writings. As you read on you will understand why I felt this way — and still do! Spontaneously written, these poems were created simply by placing pen on paper. I was tempted at times to change the wording, but each time I felt a strong resistance within me and so they are presented here in their unaltered state.

For those interested in the sequential nature of these poems, I have provided such a listing, referencing the page on which they appear. It was my thought then, as it is now, that they may help others as they did me, providing encouragement and insight for emotional growth and healing. Each poem is offered with ample space underneath should the reader wish to make notes or comments about their own reaction or thoughts at the time of their reading so as to capture them for later contemplation.

CHAPTER I

Possibilities

WHEN WAS THAT magic moment? That one thought, that one feeling, that one inspiring, connecting moment, that one event which served as a gateway to what lay ahead? When was that moment, the one which lifted me from the mundane into the land of Spirit? Was there one? If so, perhaps this was it.

December 2000, travelling to Alberta to visit family over the holiday season, my sister and I walked into the gift section of a filling station. I was captivated by the display of porcelain fairy figurines. I admired one in particular, drawn to it for some reason, as it perched delicately on a tree trunk pedestal, rising from a mossy forest bed, one leg kneeling on a limb, holding something — perhaps a blossom — in her hand, looking as though she was intoxicated by its scent. The woodiness, the lightness, her contented expression, all seemed so appealing to me.

As I was about to walk away, my sister asked me if I was really interested in having it. I told her it was a little pricey, and really, I thought, an odd purchase for a grown woman; but the child in me, enamoured by it, said "Yes!" My sister then said she would gift it to me. My heart sang as hearts do when something special has just happened. Perhaps that was the moment when Spirit began revealing itself to me, opening that small crack in the window of my soul, allowing the breeze to enter into the seemingly empty, stifled room.

Thirty-two years of marriage, tumultuous in nature, empty-nested, and having come to an end six months earlier, feeling lonely and hopeless, this fairy seemed to represent "Hope." The look of it lightened my heart, reminding me of my childhood, carefree and responsive to the moment, times in the woods seated with my back pressed into the base of a tree, sensing the fairies, the elves and the magic around me — or bounding across a meadow, free as the wild stallion I was imagining to be, hooves pounding on the turf, not a thought in my head except for my task of keeping my herd safe. Hope that what my reality had been was not necessarily all there was or could be. And, as I was to find out, so much more lay ahead, bringing real meaning to the phrase "there's always hope!"

CHAPTER II

What Was

A S THE DAYS following the break-up came one after the other, the pain of the past sank deeper and the need to sort out the future grew stronger. Life was lonely. Friends had been divided as happens when couples go their separate ways, some completely falling by the wayside, not attaching to either. Those first few months in the beginning of my new single life seem foggy now, steeped in sadness, doubt and mistrust, generated by a marriage that had been ravaged by negativity, anger, betrayal and emotional distress. I bore a heavy burden of guilt and self-loathing and wondering what was wrong with me for having allowed such things to happen. All of those years of anguish and unhappiness were being held in a place deep within me. This past was affecting me now as I struggled to move forward.

Throughout most of our thirty-two years together, my husband seemed to be on his own path, reconnecting from time to time in matters related to family life, but mostly living his life separate from mine. Why and how this marriage had become so toxic I really don't know. Conflict seemed to have been the prevailing theme in our relationship. Yes, we did make several attempts to reconcile our differences but soon after we slipped back into old ways and habits, thus undoing any good that had been accomplished, and perhaps even adding to the negativities and resentments we held toward each other. We lived a life of secrets, keeping our reality — as best we could — hidden from others, seemingly to preserve our family unit and, perhaps, our own sanity. I, for the most part, held myself responsible for the situation, being full of self-blame. I knew I had internalized the responsibility for our dysfunctional relationship—as if I was the only one responsible or in control! Throughout the years, in spite of the difficulties, I felt a strong commitment to the sanctity of the marriage, even though I was so very young and inexperienced when I took those vows.

Now, with so much pain buried deep inside of me, how could I move forward with new relationships; in making new friends, in dating, or in life for that matter? I was not able to find comfort anywhere. Workmates were kind and generous in lending me their ears; a counsellor was supportive as I spilled my feelings and emotions onto her lap, showing me these were common feelings experienced by all who go through these types of changes. In spite of all this support I continued to feel alone and isolated, clinging desperately to the words on a wall plaque I had purchased several months after the breakup. The words read: "Faith makes things possible—not easy." I had hung it where I would see it often in order to remind myself of the potential for the future, somewhat like the essence of a fairy tale which reflects hardship but gives the promise of a happy ending. If the artist who designed that plaque and who decided on those words could only know what those words meant to me! Had the moment I saw that plaque been another moment of Spirit communicating with me? In retrospect, I believe it was.

Then a colleague gave me a brochure describing a singles group in a nearby city which, as well as providing a new social network, offered a ten-week facilitated self-help group titled "Rebuilding After Your Relationship Ends." It looked exactly like what I needed—a fresh start, new people and some help in establishing myself socially. Even so, the fear of the potential hazards held me from pursuing the program. I had never considered myself to be a social person. Although I longed for close friendships, my life thus far had not produced any such potential. Childhood acquaintances had drifted away and in adulthood, friendships seemed to remain superficial and short lived, attached to particular activities of life or associated with my partner and controlled by him. This left me involved with the care of our children, the home, my job and in personal health and fitness pursuits, which I embraced as they served to escape my empty life. Now, however, life had changed; children were no longer a part of everyday life and, in fact, had lives of their own, not needing any of my attention, and nor did I want to cling to them or become an emotional burden. I wondered what I would do with the rest of my life! I was at a standstill.

As time went on, the drive to begin a new life strengthened and I knew that if I was to move forward I would need to take action. One day the will to move forward overpowered the fear of the unknown. I made the phone call to meet with the organizer of the program, joined the social group and signed up for the ten-week course! Fear of the future continued to permeate my very being but the greater fear of remaining as I was carried me forward. Now, as I recall those feelings and emotions, it is difficult to pinpoint their source. How can something that is virtually unknown generate such intense fear? It felt like I was moving into a war zone although I must confess I've never been in one! I believe my main fear was that no one would like me and that I would fail at this social stuff. Where these feelings of inadequacy came from were to be revealed later.

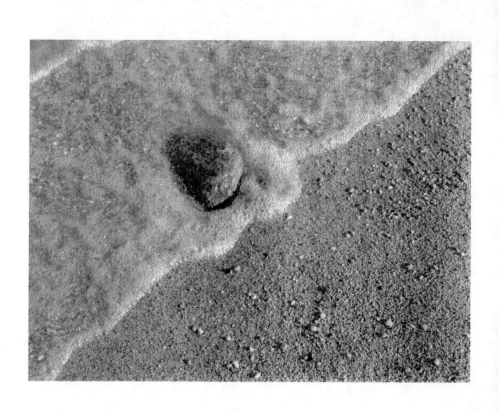

"How does one become a Butterfly?" she asked pensively.
"You must want to fly so much you are willing to give up being a
caterpillar."

Hope for the Flowers, Trina Paulus – 1972

CHAPTER III

The Turning Point

I BEGAN THE TEN-WEEK rebuilding program. Now I had an opportunity to look at who I was, how I had become this doubting, secretive person and perhaps reach some understanding of myself so that I might move forward in a more knowing way. In the weeks that followed I looked at my life — the hidden facts, that which was buried deep within, the hurt, the resentment and pain accumulated during the course of my marriage.

The journey was difficult. The group pain was tremendous, with each person slowly allowing others to catch a glimpse of the emotional place where they lived. We were encouraged to establish connections with each other, to call one another between sessions, even if only to say hello and discuss the superficial. Of course, these connections became much more than that, becoming a place of refuge, for sharing pain and progress. We were cautioned to refrain from entering into a personal relationship before completing the entire program. Without true insight it would be easy to fall back into old, undesirable habits and thought patterns which could be counterproductive in establishing a new, desirable relationship, the old not yet having been examined or replaced with new alternatives. Knowing that I travelled a great distance to attend the program after having completed a work day, one gentleman invited me to his home for dinner before a session. This was one of the most awkward times of my life, not having been alone with someone other than my spouse since my youth. I didn't know how to handle the silence and, really, how much small talk can you make? I was tense and nervous. Dinner was excellent but the evening was too uncomfortable for me, and likely for him, as we did not repeat the experience. This had been a telling evening; I knew I had a lot to learn. During my work life in the social services I was never at a loss for words but this was a different story—my personal pursuit of male companionship and affection. That evening left me feeling hopeless and ill-equipped in matters of the heart.

The turning point from despair to the possibility of happiness and joy in life came unexpectedly. On the third session of the ten-week program the subject matter of the evening was to let go of the hopes and dreams for the future which had been associated with our past lives. The task was to bring them out into the open by writing a good-bye letter. This was something that had only vaguely entered my conscious mind and during those moments I had managed to repress those thoughts quite nicely! Now, the task seemed daunting. I began to cry, unable to write down a single word. How could this be so difficult? I cried and cried! No one else in my group was crying. Until this evening, I had managed to control my emotions; in fact, really, other than fear and doubt, had not had any! I thought this program must be wrong for me. For several months now I had not even felt like crying and now to be so overwhelmed must be a backward step.

I decided to leave. The program leader encouraged me to stay and seat myself at a table behind my group; possibly reviewing the sample good-bye letter from our course material, and to circle the content that resonated with me. I looked at the list, tears flowing, and did as he suggested. I stayed the remainder of the evening. All through the drive home and through the night I cried. I cried throughout the next two days. All seemed gloom and doom. Then, the evening of the second day, as I was mowing the lawn, I started to feel the sadness lifting from my chest and the sky overhead turned a brilliant blue, as if clearing after a summer's storm. I had never smelled the fragrance of fresh cut grass as I did that evening, nor since! The memory of that moment stays fresh in my mind to this day. I finished the task with a joyful and hopeful heart. That was my turning point. My heart opened up to the world. Thereafter emotions of all sorts bubbled over, including glimpses of happiness and exuberance for life itself.

I vividly recall an evening or two later while riding my bicycle down a country highway, throwing my arms into the air and shouting

"I'm free!" into the ethers surrounding me, as though I had just been released from a long and torturous imprisonment. This would actually be an accurate description of how I had been feeling.

Now, freed from the shackles of the past, I was at liberty to take my life in any direction I wanted; although at the time I had no idea where that would lead me.

The Child Within Me

What has happened to me?
I don't understand, my emotions bubble on my surface,
almost uncontrollably . . . I feel again.
Not since childhood, memories are returning that I thought
were gone forever . . .
the ones that reflect my feelings of freedom, nature and oneness
with God and Universe . . . the starry ones,
the ones that bring fantasies to reality!
I love it and admire it . . . others think I'm insane.
Saneness . . . what is that?
I rather think I'm the sane one amongst insanity.

Reflections by Sue
July 10th, 2001 (2)

CHAPTER IV

The Healing Begins

I CONTINUED THROUGH THE program of self-discovery, learning about myself and uncovering how and why I had become this self-doubting, insecure, secretive person. The course offered in this group self-help program was that designed by Dr. Bruce Fisher. This program, guided by group facilitators who themselves were graduates of the program, acknowledges the grieving process required for the successful release of a relationship which has ended and guides participants to take an honest look at their own personal issues which may have been contributing factors. As well, the program offered support for re-establishing one's self-esteem and opportunities to acquire new, healthy ways of relating, in hopes that the past would not be repeated.

In addition to the ten-week course, I had also joined the associated singles club which offered a wide variety of group recreational and leisure activities. I began reaching out, attending as many events as I possibly could. I started having fun again after so much sorrow! I made a few new friends from the club, in particular one gal who has become the girlfriend I had always wished I'd had. She and I had the summer of our lives which neither of us will ever forget. We had come from similar backgrounds, both having married at a very young age with lives thereafter focused on work and family, and not really having had opportunity for a playful youth. We both say we lived all of our teen years in that summer, carefree and without worry for the future. Life was indeed full of adventure!

In mid-June at one of the group's singles dances I met a man. My first impressions as he ogled me from across the dance floor were not particularly favourable! He had a smug look and a rather silly grin on his face. Later, the group organizer, in his usual way of ensuring that people were mixing, asked my girlfriend and I whether the two gentlemen seated at the table behind us could join us. As the nature of the program was to foster social mixing, of course we agreed. One of these gentlemen was this man. Now what intrigued me about him was that he actually talked; something that I had so rarely experienced outside of my work environment. He also danced. I was initially drawn to him for these two reasons. It was exciting for me to finally find someone who seemed interesting and was interested in me. The attraction was incredible. And he was so different from my previous partner!

After our first encounter he gave me his telephone number—not asking for mine—and left our future, if there was to be one, in my hands. The idea of pursuing him was frightening, and yet I knew that this could be the opportunity I was looking for, someone outside of my own community and not linked to my past life. I found the courage to make the call. I was nervous and anxious as to whether he would even remember me. He didn't until I identified myself. Then we made plans to go to a movie and found the attraction just as strong on our second meeting. And so we began to date.

This seemed to be the spark I needed to light my inner flame and connection with Spirit. Our relationship gave me many opportunities for self-discovery and emotional awakening. I found myself struggling with old ways of thinking and feeling. The bite of a few words and the drama that unfolded in my mind was almost unbelievable and unbearable and yet without these triggers the healing could not have taken place. "Demons" began to be released from inside of me. I began to figuratively refer to this man as my Demon Slayer since he became the spark that triggered my awareness; allowing Spirit to do the rest. Demons of the mind, who knows their origin, demons that smother and restrict our growth, causing us to stay in our safe protective shell. Some of them originate from our own personal journey, some from others' stories, and some from the lives of our parents and perhaps even the story of all humanity dating back to the beginning. Each of us needs to release our demons if we are to fly and be joyful. My relationship with this man became the strike point for revealing my demons. It was frightening and yet exciting as I ventured forward. Something seemed to be guiding my experiences. I can only attribute these to Spirit and God. Wondrous coincidences and lessons of life, insights, revelations, healing and hope appeared in places I would not have thought to look.

The Demon Slayer

Past demons, we all have them.
Mine spring up when I least expect them.
Like predators in the night.
Everyone needs a demon slayer to survive . . .
No, to thrive.
You were mine . . . reassurance . . .
you couldn't do anything else then,
you did the best you could,
you're fun . . . playful . . .
accepting for who and what I am.
The pain is leaving.
Thank-you, my demon slayer.

Reflections by Sue
June 23, 2001 (2)

The Crows

A small remark . . . how could it raise such an alarm?
The crows have been stepping on your face . . . what?
Fear welled within me, the past relived . . .
silent rejection . . . never again, insignificant, torn to pieces . . .
emotional turmoil, insignificant.
Oh please, not again.
Those terrible crows, they've been on your face . . . oh?
Acceptance, yes, respect?
Yes . . . Oh Joy!
It will be ok.

Reflections by Sue
June 23, 2001 (1)

CHAPTER V

Emotional Growth

MUCH WAS REVEALED to me during those few months; truths about life, love, humanity and the workings of the unseen mind became a path of healing for my wounded soul. I found that situations, which in my past would have seemed trivial and irrelevant, evoked ideas and insights I had never thought of before. My perceptions seemed eerily acute, surreal, and wonderfully alive, causing me to feel as though I was the observer of my perceptions rather than the one having the experience. This allowed me to bring an objective look at what was happening.

I began a series of spontaneous writings and poems, short and focused on the thought, feeling and revelation of the moment, referring to them as "Reflections by Sue." It was both interesting and alarming to me that those with whom I shared my insights and writings spoke of how they resembled the works of modern poets such as Margaret Attwood, Carol Shields and of Biblical verse. I found myself resenting these comparisons since it felt as though they were questioning my declared inspiration for this work, suggesting that the works of others may be my inspirational source rather than direct influence from Spirit. I felt comfort knowing that I was not really familiar with those works, not having spent any time studying the Bible or reading the works of the authors mentioned – in fact had spent little time reading any works other than for my occupation. I was grateful for this and felt again that Spirit had been responsible for my having turned away from literature after having been an avid reader in my youth, feeling that this too had been part of the master plan! Knowing that I did not have these influences, I could say with full certainty that my experiences were raw, living proof of the spontaneous movement of Spirit in helping me to heal.

During this time my emotions were on full display—from sadness, despair, and melancholy to awe, disbelief, excitement, joy and delight, but mostly joy. I could not contain the joy I felt! Some of those who had known me well before this awakening commented on the changes they saw in me and asked "do you have to be so happy?" I simply was not able to contain the joy I felt in my heart. Even when experiencing sadness, the joy seeped out and revealed itself, leaving me feeling uplifted rather than disheartened. This joy seemed to be linked to the gratitude which I felt toward Spirit for guiding what was taking place and for the process which Spirit was using for my healing, revealing so much to me through ordinary and extraordinary means. I found that my healing "Spirit guides" showed up when I least expected them and came in many different forms! Past experiences which had created my internal truths—truths which governed my thoughts and reactions—often came into question. I felt as though I was discovering a whole new world! So with an air of openness and curiosity as to what the next moment might bring, I marched forward on an adventure of being!

The future with my new found male companion was exciting and unpredictable. I was smitten with this affair of the heart. However, having been forewarned of the dangers of first relationships after divorce during the group work, I was not naive as to the uncertainty of such relationships and so constantly reminded myself to be mentally open to all and any possibility. During these early days, even though he seemed to be quite interested in me, I often received subtle—and not so subtle—messages of uncertainty about the potential for anything other than a short term relationship.

I found myself on an emotional roller coaster ride, sometimes rocketing skyward and the next instant plummeting wildly downward. Again, although I felt these emotions with extreme intensity at the time, I also seemed to be observing them at a distance, being acutely aware of all that was happening to me and the effect they were having on my "self" and yet feeling crazily detached!

The value of such experiences, the role they were playing in my healing and their role for all of humanity was revealed to me in the content of several of my poems. Apparently our relationships with others—not only those with risk for loss, but those which end in loss—play an integral part in the human experience, opening new doors for emotional growth and development, and allowing us to reach our full human potential. As painful as they might seem at the time, without these types of experiences our emotional growth would be stunted and limited. As the saying goes *'Tis better to have loved and lost, than never to have loved at all!'* (In Memoriam A.H.H., Alfred Lord Tennyson, 1850) Taking risk, and even losing something precious to us, it seems, is necessary for the opening of these doors to growth; such experiences serve to strengthen and expand us on our life journey.

The Day of Mourning—Lost Love

A figure of speech
I said to he. That four letter word.
But it was not to be. Lost Love . . .
so the day that followed became
my day of mourning.
Don't be sad . . . morning is
a good time of day . . .
I wore my mourning dress . . . that
respectful, delightful dress
that always makes me feel I've given my utmost in respect to
that person
who lies there in front of me, still & cold.
The one that makes me think of all the positive things
about that person, admiration, thank-fullness to
have known that individual and in the future
evokes those memories again . . .
keeping those fond memories alive . . . no pain, just
pleasant thoughts.
I love this dress . . . so many people are enfolded in its field of
flowers . . . the sparkly
glass buttons . . .
this dress has been with me for over a decade . . .
allowing me to cling to all those people I loved, but who are gone in
body . . .
and now have a spiritual existence against my skin,
flowing with me each time I take a step.
What a fine dress!

Reflections by Sue,
July 10, 2001 (1)

Wanting to Feel

Feelings are a good thing.
Feelings remind you you're alive.
Why avoid it then?
Even an earthworm responds to a stimulus and is not denied.
Am I not at least a creature
worthy of touch and risk?
Feelings and exposure, it's what I've
needed.
A vacuum is worthless and does not honour the feelings and
expressions endowed to humanity.
Please don't cut me off from risk!
I need it . . . I've been so deprived and isolated in my lonely world.
Let me feel . . . sadness, laughter, tears.
Feel the pain, good pain . . . not the pain of my past,
controlling, abusing pain . . . pain that hides you from the world and
your right to life.
Please let me live and feel the pain that real love and caring
and kindness can bring.
Thank-you my Demon Slayer.
Happiness Always,

Reflections by Sue
July 10, 2001 (3)

The Sentinel

What was that signal? The warning
light glowed . . . people meeting people,
other friends . . . girlfriends . . . what
was that signal?
It was the one I had been waiting for . . . the sign
that alerted me to the end.
How could I have known it would come like this?
Really, the first sign,
then retraction . . . relationship . . . we have one?
That other signal, sharing what with my children?
A vacation? What was that?
Oh, so confused . . . it's haunting me.
My emotions swell and recede, up & down, up & down,
like the ocean at tide time.
What is he meaning . . . independent,
dependent . . . who said anything about dependency,
not I . . . that is not in my meaning of love . . . is it in yours?

Reflections by Sue
July 10, 2001 (4)

CHAPTER VI

Lessons from Spirit

FILLED WITH A new sense of optimism, joy and anticipation of things to come, I began a new adventure; a new way of being. Somehow I instinctively knew that I needed to open up to others so that I might be able to truly live life. In my weary world of secrets I had become isolated and mistrustful of everyone, fearing that any opening would lead to more pain. My wall of silence, which had protected me for so long, needed to be torn down. I now realized I was not an island and I, too, needed to receive as well as give. Now I realized that the path to healing was to break my silence, to connect with others, to share what had happened to me and to accept other's gifts. Where before I would have lacked self-confidence, fearing the resulting interaction, I now set my fears aside and pressed forward into new frontiers of the heart and soul. In fact, I can honestly say those fears had all but disappeared! I spoke to people whenever the opportunity presented itself; in shopping lines, in waiting rooms, extending a helping hand wherever I could, accepting help from others and exposing myself to socially "risky" situations intentionally.

Isolation

A Silent World.
Quiet, paining, isolating silence.
Watching, waiting . . . for what?
The demon lurks . . .
chastising the words that come from my mouth.
Deeper I sink into the silence . . . silence to keep peace, silence
to keep from screaming,
silence to bury the demon deeper and deeper.
Oh, the silence explodes in my head!
So damaging, sadness overwhelms me.
Now I laugh, I ramble, I scream,
I whisper, I sing, I hum, I dance.
I speak to strangers and acquaintance alike!
No longer a silent, rejecting world.
People accept me, they like me, they love me!
Thanks to all my Spirit guides who have rescued me from the deep.
Those who were with me from the beginning.
Those I met while I waited in lines at the bank and while shopping.
Waiting no longer to connect with humanity.
Thank-you to the stranger at the Forks for sharing our moment.
Thank-you person in the shopping line.
Thank-you Rebecca at the Clinic.
And the Mom with the child.
Thank-you for making me part of the world.
No more isolation.

Reflections by Sue
July 12, 2001 (1)

Bittersweet

Bittersweet creeps into our lives.
Not the way we would recognize it,
but bit by bit, edging its way, pushing
aside the sweetness we once knew.
The sweetness, the innocence of life,
that part of you that clings to your spirit,
like nectar to a bee, necessary for its life.
That part of you that believes in the fairies, in the angels,
in the freedom of spirit.
Bittersweet begins to control your thoughts,
your words and all you do.
Bred through anger, it only leaves when the anger is gone.
Anger is a lingering emotion—now it's here, now it's not!
Feel it! Know the enemy, purge yourself of it and
again you will feel the fairies, the angels and your free spirit
will fly!
Happy landing to all.

Reflections by Sue
July 12, 2001 (3)

I was awestruck by what was happening to me, knowing that I was not in control as evidenced by the synchronicity that surrounded me. I knew that this 'awakening' was a gift from God. I had no idea how things would unfold, only that I was on an amazing journey, so much different than my life before. I continued asking and thanking God for guidance, realizing that God was leading me on this journey and that this God-force was my primary Spirit guide, responsible for placing all the others on my path.

I found that helpers were all around me. As an example, while shopping at a Farmer's Market, I was offered assistance to carry my purchases to my car by a young female employee. At first I declined, however it came into my thoughts that to continue with my independent attitude would not benefit me or the other person. I then changed my decision and accepted her help.

On the walk to the car I explained how I had been independent for so long and that one way of helping me to connect with others would be to accept some help from other people, not to limit the connections I make with others. I needed to see the potential for new relationships that could evolve from such interactions. She smiled. I asked if she understood what I meant by that and she replied "Yes, I can." The expression on her face and the tone of her voice as she said those words told me that indeed she did!

I felt uplifted by this exchange and knew that I had received a great lesson from Spirit—to be open to others, mindful of what others can offer me and not only of what I could offer them—that healing lies in the connections with others; that we are all on a journey of discovery in this thing called humanity; and that in order to discover something new one needs to trust and have faith in the great unfolding.

I felt like a different person. Not only did I feel different, those who knew me attested to that.

A New Me

People say I'm not the person I was.
I don't know, sometimes I feel the same.
Other times I feel like a new beginning.
Like my life is just starting now . . . and
I feel.
No longer looking in from the outside.
But at peace with my new task in life.
Knowing that I can help others.
God, give me the strength to carry on and
see what I need to do!
Although I do see it clearly now
and I will not fail you.
Peace to all, that is the final hurrah!

Reflections by Sue
July 12, 2001 (2)

CHAPTER VII

Trust Renewed

M Y TRUST HAD been shattered over the years: trust in God, trust in human nature and trust in myself. Thankfully, this too was included in my lessons from Spirit. The betrayals and negativity of my marriage had left me distrustful of everyone and had caused me to retreat deep within myself, afraid to share any genuine feelings with anyone, fearing ridicule at some later time.

This shell outwardly reflected as a strong independence and self-reliance. I came to believe that the only one I could count on was myself and therefore I created a wall of strength (silence) between myself and others. Without help from God, from Spirit, I don't believe I would ever have come out of my shell. My new found male friend, I felt, had been situated in my life so that healing experiences could be placed on my path. He became a portal to self-discovery; an instrument for my enlightenment and healing. As I refer to him in my writings — a Demon Slayer — bringing an end to the silent influence of my past partner, bringing an end to my confined thinking of the past, providing hope and meaning for the future and value to my existence. The unfolding of these events was amazing and mystical, and, for me, provided evidence for the presence of a greater plan.

Lessons from Spirit . . . the classroom

The Two Wine Glasses

One evening I arrived at my new found male friend's home unaccompanied by him, now having been given my own key as he worked into the late evening. As I stepped into the kitchen I noticed two used wine glasses on the counter. My heart sank. A foreboding feeling overcame me, striking fear in my heart as I struggled with the meaning of that. Imagine, two wine glasses evoking such a response! What a story I was creating in my mind. Mistrust, betrayal, the ending of this affair of the heart, more loneliness — the past relived. However, as the evening unfolded it came to me that this very type of response is about control and ownership of others, attitudes that reflect meeting one's own needs and not valuing the free choice and will of others, characteristics which I had abhorred in my previous partner. I now realized my current thoughts, emotions and conclusions were based on my past experience. This did not necessarily mean anything. I understood that my current actual pain was based on a fictional story created in my head, not on the facts surrounding this situation. It most likely reflected an automatic reaction based on the experiences associated with my previous marital relationship. I then knew that trust must be the beginning basis for all relationships, that for anything good to happen, trust must be the underpinning of all actions and reactions. And so the following poem ensued:

Mistrust

The dirtiest word of all.
The word that brings the end to everything.
I'm so sorry this is what has happened to me.
The thing that he stole from the depth of my soul,
little by little.
He stole my ability to be faithful, true and trusting of others,
I realize that now.
How will I reconnect with my humanity, that innate
connection necessary for survival of the species.
The ability to have faith and trust in your fellow man,
that others will only do what is best for all and for you.
Oh, how I long to trust and have faith in others again!
A beginning state.
I want and long for this basic need;
to start from a position of trust.
Please God, give this back to me.
Forgive me.
It's such an injustice I have done to you.
He lurks at my every turn.
Please forgive me.

Reflections by Sue
July 15, 2001 (4)

Mixed Emotions

I now realize that the
change within me must come
from different positions . . .
sadness, fear, melancholy
hate, love, joy, happiness and so on.
Whatever state humanity is capable of.
My Demon Slayer helped me with this understanding.
It seems like such a long journey . . . somewhat like Alice
in Wonderland.
Where everything seems like one thing at one moment,
then suddenly it's something else.
What a roller coaster ride!
Why would I think that having my task set out
before me would give me immunity from the human state?
This is mine to bear and I must do the work, as I tell others.
Will the work ever be done?
I don't think so.
I'm getting tired.

Reflections by Sue
July 15, 2001 (5)

Possessiveness

The breaker of relationships.
The destroyer of the freedom of each.
I know this.
The leader, though, is mistrust, the giver of fear.
Mistrust brings the need to be forever close in body.
This is not in my definition of love!
And so trust, trusting myself,
trusting others will become my ocean bed.
Like the corals of the sea and wonders of the deep, so
vulnerable to the abuse of others.
Trust will underlay all my interactions with people.
Perhaps with a little sense of caution,
keeping safety of body in sight,
so that I will be able to finish my work.
Trust leads to 'freedom of each', as in my definition of love.
Mistrust leads to fear and possessiveness and endings.
Thank-you, my demon-slayer, for being strong
for me on my journey, sheltering me from a
long, painful path of discover,
enduring this pain no longer.

Reflections by Sue
July 16, 2001 (1)

Through the Looking-Glass

And so having resolved the issue of the two wine glasses, I settled in to spend the evening by myself awaiting my male friend's late arrival home. I decided to manicure my nails and apply nail polish, which I did. Then, still having a great deal of time to while away, I decided to spend some time exploring my new found partner's book shelves. He had a wonderful collection of books, in particular, a special edition collection published by "The Heritage Club." Each of these books were beautifully crafted and bound and further protected by a color coordinated hard cover sleeve. My friend had signed each volume on the blank first inside page, showing me the personal value he placed on them. Some of the titles I recognized, others I did not. I decided to read one with which I was not familiar and so at random I picked out *Through the Looking – Glass*. Although the title sounded vaguely familiar, I did not know of what this story told. Later I was to find out that my choice had not really been so random.

First, I read the insert which described the considerable lengths that had been taken by the Heritage Club to reproduce the original drawings done for the book's first release in 1871 by the very much admired and sought after illustrator of the day, John Tenniel. As I read this accounting, I realized that not only was this collection valuable, it was probably irreplaceable and so I became extra cautious in my handling of the book. Continuing to read through the leaflet, I found the story of the author's personal struggle in seeking perfection for his books – including his conflict with his illustrator – very interesting.

The leaflet also explained the history as to how it was that Dodgson (pen name Lewis Carroll), who was by education and career a mathematical lecturer, came to write this book as well as his first book of this kind *Alice In Wonderland*. Now, that book I was familiar with and so I thought this book might be quite to my taste! (You may recall that in the poem which immediately precedes this situation, I stated I was feeling somewhat like Alice in Wonderland, where everything seemed like one thing at one moment, and suddenly it was something else!) Then, just as I began to read the actual story, calamity struck! The book slipped from my hands and, in attempting to prevent it falling to the floor, one of my fingers slid over the first page and, to my horror, it left a stripe of nail polish, a fine line, directly under my friend's signature!

Oh the alarm, the self-recrimination. I had been so careful and in spite of all my precautions, I had damaged someone else's most valuable possession. My mind leapt to my previous experiences, how I had been found guilty and responsible countless times by my previous partner for events that were not at all in my control, resulting in a barrage of verbal abuse and attack on my character. The nightmare returned along with all of the feelings and emotions of that time. Now the question, how to deal with this present situation? Well, as I had come to believe that honesty is always the best policy and that errors one makes are best dealt with at the time one realizes one has been made, I decided that I would confess as soon as he came home.

And so I tried to sleep for a while. Then he arrived. With great trepidation and my heart beating rapidly in my chest, I told him what had happened. His reply, "Well, so you've put your mark on it!" Nothing else—no verbal attack, no angry tone, no character assassination. In fact, realizing I hadn't finished reading the book, he encouraged me to take it home to finish it, continuing to trust me with the care of this book! I was emotionally taken aback by his almost uncaring attitude to what had happened, his only concern being that I hadn't completed reading the book! And so I took the book home to finish it.

The real lesson and healing moment of this incident came to me very suddenly in the opening chapter of the book as Alice entertains climbing through the mirror—the looking-glass—and does so in order see what's in that other house. In fact she found that everything there was "as different as possible." When I read those words I had an immediate epiphany, that in fact, everything that was now happening to me would be very different from before and that indeed, I was on an adventure, an Adventure with Spirit! The hand of an "outside force" was evident and undeniable as similar synchronicities continued to appear at every turn and when I was most in need.

CHAPTER VIII

The Assignment Revealed

THE SIGNIFICANT MOMENT that led me to the sharing of my story came out of the blue. Late one night my new found male friend and I were having our usual telephone conversation. I was sharing some of the agonizing moments of my past and the pangs of remorse and regret I was feeling as I questioned whether by remaining in my marriage I had actually failed my son who had frequently been the brunt of his father's misplaced anger. My friend, in his attempt to reassure me, told me about some of his childhood experiences and family history. He had been one of ten children when his mother had died and so his father became a single parent for a period of time. He reflected that taking care of this many children had not been easy for his father and that to maintain peace and order in such a large household was extremely difficult but necessary. Therefore if a disruption occurred, his father would need to resolve the issue quickly. The children learned that, even though they might be innocent, it would be best to give a false confession so as to end the matter. My friend seemed to be excusing his father based on the challenges he was facing in being a single parent with so many children. I was appalled at his attitude, always having been a believer in justice and fairness. I was angry at him for accepting this as a necessary evil in his upbringing. I went to sleep that night feeling sad and despondent about the situation.

The next morning was to be the beginning of a new adventure with Spirit. I arose as usual, preparing myself for the work day, still stewing about the conversation of the night before. Justice had always been my touchstone and as far back as I could remember, in both my personal and professional life, and as far back as my childhood memories would take me, I had used fairness as a measure in making judgements and decisions. The next moment remains vivid in my mind to this day. I was standing in my bathroom facing the mirror and, suddenly, a jolt of energy—lightning-like—struck me from above, entered my crown and moved quickly down through my torso, into my arms and legs, and left though the soles of my feet. It was unlike anything I had ever felt before! In that same instant, an amazing conclusion came into my mind and words sprang out of my mouth for which I could not account: "That's it! I'm supposed to write three books. That's why I'm here!" Then, I had a sudden urge to take a pen to paper and what happened next was truly miraculous. "The Secrets That We Keep" quickly flowed onto the paper before me.

The Secrets That We Keep

We tell our children . . . secrets . . . such lies . . . tell all . . . tell those you trust.
Get help . . . things can get better, tell all . . . you're ok . . . you're not responsible.
Then we practice the lie.
We keep the secret within us, the mistrust, the hurt, the pain caused by others to our souls.
How could we let such a thing happen!
It seems so obvious now . . . the secret that was within us, both knowing and yet revealing nothing.
The secret slipped deeper and deeper into ourselves until the secret felt like the truth . . . and owned the rights of a truth.
The only difference being that truth brings "light" to your life!
Secrets bring pain, sorrow and more lies and more secrets.
Secrets revealed bring pain first, then they lay there in a pile . . .
ready to be examined . . . one-by-one . . . and the process is long and difficult.
But the end, Oh, such Peace, such Freedom, new Life!
I'm telling the whole world about my Secrets.
Joy to the World and my Spirit guides who brought me here.

Reflections by Sue,
July 11, 2001 (1)

The Web of Lies

There they are, neatly meshed into your lives.
Living things, controlling what you do and say,
what you share with others.
Why bother you say, what good would it do?
Truth for all, a challenge to you!
A challenge to disentangle yourself from those lies, the web,
so sticky, it clings to you, not wanting to release you.
Be brave and strong and pull away,
Happiness lies beyond.

Reflections by Sue
July 11, 2001 (2)

Control

Liberty is so elusive.
Subtle control. Why, what about the human state
brings this desire—to hold power over another?
To push pain into your soul, squeezing out your goodness.
And the anger builds and eats you, stealing your life force,
until it feels like a thing living inside of you,
affecting your connection with others.
Why, who can answer this question? No one can,
no one can.
Live and let live is my belief.

Reflections by Sue
July 11, 2001 (3)

This moment of realization—that I was to write three books—was very powerful! The words were not my own. The energy surge seemed to be responsible and yet it was my own voice that spoke. At the same time I had a distinct feeling that the books I was to write were about helping others who were dealing with the pains of abuse, of abandonment and betrayal, and even for those who were responsible for those pains. I had no idea how this would come to be or what I would be writing about. I had never aspired to be a writer nor did I feel qualified to become one.

This was a "Big" assignment considering I had very little knowledge or experience in this area! But I quickly came to realize that all I needed to do was accept the assignment and commit to telling my story; Spirit and God would give me the content. The truths revealed that day were both alarming and yet so comforting. Insights and messages for healing and recovery continued to flow in the form of poems. They said everything that needed to be said, with wisdom and clarity.

Although at the time I felt inadequate for the task, upon reflection I probably had much more knowledge and understanding than I realized. My mother had had a tragic childhood, losing both parents one day of each other during an epidemic at age ten and then she was placed in a home separate from her younger brother—and only sibling. During the time she was 'in care' she suffered both physical and sexual abuse at the hands of her caregivers. Then she married my father, who continued a pattern of dishonour and disrespect with his philandering ways, frequently leaving her financially distressed for periods of time. He had perpetuated those feelings of abandonment which had begun with the death of her parents at such a tender, young age.

Now I realized it was not only for myself, for my pain, but for the hurt felt by others, for my mother who suffered in silence, for all others who suffer in silence and for those who were not, as yet, aware of their plight—for whom I was being given this assignment. My long career in supporting people living with a mental disability had shown me the many sides of humanity and a sampling of the atrocities endured by the most vulnerable in society, inflicted by those preying on their vulnerability. The issues underlying this deep, dark shadow side of humanity, the effects and the underlying motivation behind such hurtful actions, along with the prescription for bettering ourselves, was also to be revealed to me. All of these are presented in the following chapters.

Clarity

At sleep, the thoughts mingle and blend in my mind,
individual at first, caressing each other until they become one.
Clarity from doubt; thoughts and ideas massaging each other,
blending gently to be transformed into new thoughts,
a new idea.
This wonderful transformation bringing clarity
to my mind, bringing stories to be told, things to behold!
The mind, the wonder of humanity.
Follow your mind, it's a wondrous thing!
Let it have a life of its own.

Reflections by Sue
July 15, 2001 (1)

The Greatness Within You

It comes in a flash!
So quickly it frightens you.
A certainty that strikes you at your very core,
enveloping you in its excitement.
Give it reverence.
It is your work that has been assigned to you.
Hold it high, like a flame.
It is what you've waited for all of your life.
A gift from God, from the Universe,
from the World that cries out for help from you.
You will be victorious.
How could you fail?
Failure is not a word worthy of mention.
There is no failure in this assignment.
Only victory to be had.
Each will have their greatness revealed to them.
I have mine.
Be patient, you must suffer and be groomed for your task.
Power to the Universe!
Sweeping away evil & disrespect.

Reflections by Sue
July 15, 2001 (3)

From that moment on, I had a much clearer understanding of what was happening. I had been chosen to share my story with others, for the benefit of others, to help those who were suffering in silence; for those who did not, as yet, know their pain which was buried so deeply in their body and mind; and even for those who caused the suffering of others, since they too, had secrets buried so deeply within them. I now felt that everything in my life had happened in order to bring me to this place. I now viewed my past pain as having been a necessary experience for this miraculous awakening. The feeling of finally knowing why I was here on this earth was a great relief and joy!

As a young child I recall often gazing into the mirror, examining my face and asking the questions: "Who am I, what am I, and why am I here?" Having my earthly assignment revealed brought understanding as to why I was on this "insightful journey" and brought meaning to all of my past experiences and to my life itself! It felt as though something large and extremely important was happening which I referred to as one's greatness revealed. "The Greatness Within You" shares this experience. I felt an overwhelming feeling of gratitude towards God for giving me this assignment; this opportunity to bring "light" into the lives of others.

I asked for help in keeping my path clear, asking for strength to resist the influence of others that might cause me to stray from my path, although I could not see how that could possibly happen! My faith in God and in the power of God—whom I referred to as my greatest Spirit guide—was restored. I found myself wonderfully engulfed in a state of absolute joy. Others who knew me saw this change in me and remarked upon it.

My poem "They Say" reflects upon the changes others observed in me and to what I attributed those changes. It was amazing to feel so much joy and peace and love in my heart for everyone and everything. I truly was in love with life itself!

They Say

They say I look alive,
the people who have known me forever.
They say I have a sparkle & spirit in my eyes,
clear windows to my soul;
the dull grey covering gone!
They say I've a different attitude
in recent weeks.
They say they like the change.
I give energy; I don't take it from them.
What a marvellous change when
one knows their purpose in life,
understands their place in time.
Shedding the anger, the pain, the hurt,
the feelings of injustice.
And understanding why it was
necessary to endure.
A happy day!

Reflections by Sue
July 19, 2001

CHAPTER IX

Revelations of Life

I BEGAN BEING BOMBARDED with an almost continuous flow of information about the healing process and about the role of others in this process and about life itself. Revelations about life's purpose and human nature sprang into my mind, sometimes triggered by a thought or by an interaction with someone and often out of nowhere! Somehow, I knew that what I was receiving would be very important at a later time. I was not able to keep up with writing down everything that was coming into my consciousness as the flow was so continuous and happening at the most inopportune times, including while I was driving. I began to carry a small voice-activated tape recorder. This recording has proven remarkably useful as I now, some ten years later, sit down to write this book.

During a seven day span—between the 13th and 19th of July, 2001—I learned that what was, could no longer be; isolation, silence and disconnect with humanity allows pain to worsen. Reconnection to people is one of the solutions to our personal problems and to the world's problems. Healing can only happen through the connection with others and the sharing of the human experience. Theories and ideas on what motivates people to bring harm to others came into my awareness. Although I realized these ideas were not entirely new in the field of psychology, they felt new, alive and real to me as they arose from my own mind, a place inside of me, energized and full of knowing, rather than from a dry textbook interpretation or from an intellectual study of the topic. Perhaps these ideas and notions were reaching me from those theorists from the past, through the timeless realm.

I likened what I was experiencing to Abraham Maslow's notion of self-actualization, where at a point upon which our most basic of needs have been met, we are inspired to make a meaningful contribution to the world. During the course of my career in serving people with mental disabilities, I had found Maslow's hierarchy of needs very helpful, both in planning services and for understanding my clients' behaviour. Within this context of human motivation, it was easy to see why a person who had an extremely challenging disability and who so obviously needed assistance would reject the help of others and strive toward independence. In so doing they would often subject themselves to great risk, generating much anxiety and fear in their family and caregivers. This framework, I felt, offered a guidepost for anyone on the human journey and acknowledged our mutual needs not only for the basics of life, but also for our many emotional and social needs. I believed that anyone, regardless of ability or disability, given the right circumstance, could and would reach their potential — self-actualization.

Now, I surmised that the process of self-actualization may well be how we receive our life assignments. It seemed to me that this model for viewing the human journey deserved much greater consideration and study, in particular as it was unravelling in my life at the time. I was overjoyed at coming to this realization since I had found this model so useful in my professional work. Now, not only were my beliefs being affirmed, but with this personal experience, I was truly able to acknowledge the spiritual component as well.

A distinct feeling of "Oneness" arose within me. I felt connected, with a sense of good will and caring for everybody and everything. These feelings, although not as pronounced, continue to this day! I was filled with gratitude for all that had happened and was happening. Although I acknowledged the depth of what had happened to me during my marriage, I held no malice toward my previous partner and viewed my past distress as a necessary experience for this miraculous awakening and the setting out of my life work.

This connectedness feeling seems to have played a pivotal role in how I viewed life prior to, and since that time. Previously, I held the belief that being spiritual (religious) meant that I would need to separate myself from the society in which I lived. This pained me a great deal since this would mean abandoning so many people I loved and, it had seemed, life itself! It appeared to me to be a bleak and lonely path. I now saw that exactly the opposite was true. Now, with this epiphany, it seemed that this journey of spirit is about connecting with others — not about separation — and not a matter of giving up the world, but of being a part of whatever is happening, and partaking of the world, being guided by your own morality and ethical parameters. In fact, the instruction was clear — do not disengage yourself from what is happening around you, but engage and connect with others, the focus to be very much on 'interdependency.' So this life than is not to be about separation but about living your life in connection with others, enjoying your existence and all that the world has to offer. Previous to this I had felt a 'disconnect' with the world, rather like an outsider looking in. Now I felt 'of this world' — connected, involved, feeling joy in the things around me, in nature and in people, finding comfort and reassurance all around me, feeling joy in the existence of God and the assignment that had been given to me.

"Nothing changes until something moves." Albert Einstein
"And the thing that must move is me. What part of me has to move first? My mind." Dr. Wayne W. Dyer

CHAPTER X

Human Frailty

THESE REVELATIONS OF course would not have been complete without acknowledging the darker side of life, the reason that we treat each other in less than caring ways. Why is it, even when we know the difference between right and wrong, even when we know what is just or unjust, fair or unfair, we still may choose hurtful actions, actions which inflict pain on another, actions which are meant to control others against their will, and which may result in outcomes which are not in the other person's best interest? This too was revealed to me.

Underlying and motivating these actions is a desire to meet our own needs through the lives of others rather than doing the work for and within ourselves. This is the human state, the state that we have been given, the frailty of humanity. This is what lies behind "evil" deeds; this is the power behind actions and behaviours which may be hurtful and cause others to suffer.

Added to this are the temptations and draws of the material world, which is so honoured and even worshiped in our present society. Be aware that the material world reflects the selfish bits, the bits that can separate us from our connection with others and from conscious choice making, and can slowly steal our personal power, our connection with Spirit, ever so silently and unknowingly, like a thief in the night!

The task for us is to unseat these other powers; to look at our actions and see them for what they are, choices serving only the self, coming out of fear and want. We have the ability, the personal power, to make other choices—caring choices, choices to do good toward others, choices which honour and respect the human state in yourself and in others.

This is the first step for those who abuse and dishonour others, to acknowledge that they have been looking primarily at their own needs and not considering the needs of others. Upon recognising this, the abuser, previously unaware of what was motivating his/her behaviour, now has the power to change, to reconnect with humanity and begin the healing process.

The opening of the Secret Box is as important for them as for those who are on the receiving end of the abuse, and, in fact, is important for society as a whole if we are to move toward a place of peace. It is important that the 'lies' are exposed for what they are and that they do not become a hallmark to which we orient our lives. Much of our personal and societal anger evolves from thoughtless actions, actions which do not consider the needs of others. Only by listening to the hearts and minds of others and acknowledging the needs of others can we hope to come to a place of peace within ourselves and in the world.

Acknowledging the frailty of humanity, acknowledging that we all have this weakness, that this is a universal human characteristic to which we can—and do—all fall victim, gives us all hope, hope for the possibility of change and recovery of everyone, hope for a better tomorrow!

The Frailty of Humanity

In our weakened state
we fail to see things clearly.
Things change moment to moment within us.
The world pressing us for decisions . . .
but there are none.
Searching for the answer,
the answer eludes us.
The mind weak and thus the body & soul also.
The frailty of Humanity.
Strive toward strength,
strength of mind will
determine your destiny.

Reflections by Sue
July 15, 2001 (2)

The Good and the Bad—Struggles of the Mind

There is good and bad in all of us.
It's a matter of "will" as to which you choose.
Your choice decides what is revealed—good or evil.
The decisions we make can be
selfish and self-serving.
The choice, your path,
is your own to choose.
As a child you saw and felt the choices of others.
You felt joy, happiness or
suffering and pain from their choices.
You now are an adult, having
your own power to make choices.
Make the ones you want, but
want the ones you make!
And feel comfortable in your own skin.

Reflections by Sue,
July 16, 2001 (2)

.

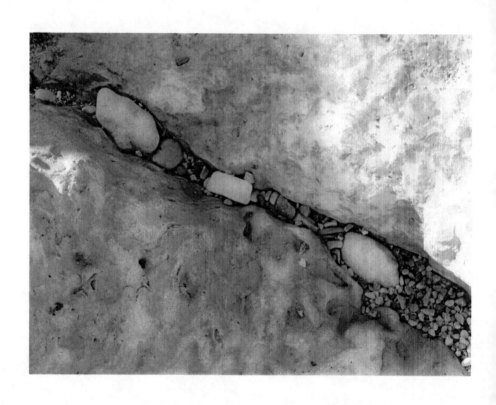

CHAPTER XI

Supporting Spirit

I T IS ONE thing to realize one's purpose, to know what is expected, but quite another to accept the assignment and to maintain your strength and resolve to ensure its completion. Thankfully a number of strategies, truths and supporting aspects to help us along the way were also channelled to me during this time. These have provided lifeblood to me when doubt crept in, as it surely will for everyone, and have strengthened me when I was feeling unworthy or ill-equipped to complete my assignment. I'm certain that you too will find these helpful and strengthening on your journey.

The messages I received revealed what is truly important on this search for meaning, to the discovery of one's purpose and to the fulfillment of the assignment. Factors which interfered with these goals were referred to as 'enemies of the soul.' These enemies of consciousness — to the awareness of what is really important — lie all around us. Society places these enemies at every turn of our lives, tempting us to make 'unconscious' decisions. These enemies have the power to hold us from gaining the strength we need to hold to our purpose and fulfill our destiny. We must shed light onto these enemies, so that they can be seen for what they really are. Early in our lives, we are not able to recognize these, but as we evolve, clarity starts and then we are able to make our choices around this understanding of what is good and what is not.

With your assignment in mind, it is now important to be **discerning of your path**, to make insightful decisions, being ever watchful for that which may be helpful and that which may lead you astray. Clearly define both what you are fighting for and what you are fighting against. Bringing such clarity to your mission will simplify the journey and provide you with the guidance you need to make the right decisions.

Of particular importance is to **resist becoming caught up in the material world** with the focus of striving for the accumulation of material goods. This ultimately diverts people from the spiritual path. However, neither is it helpful to totally reject that world since that would be interpreted as your having an aloof stance — an outsider stance — thereby risking the loss of your credibility in a world that cries out for what you have to offer!

In order to connect with the world, it is important to be seen as 'of the world' and not as separate from the world. I concluded that I had the necessary characteristics, background and abilities to be sensitive to most people's situations, having come from an impoverished upbringing, living as an ethnic outsider in the community where I grew up and now, in adulthood, being a mother, a grandmother, and a professional living in relative prosperity, supported by peer recognition and respect.

Throughout the more prosperous years of my life, I had questioned this societal drive toward materialism, its meaning and my own personal resistance to this seemingly useless, wasteful and trivial aspect of the western lifestyle. I now felt as though all of this had been given to me as grooming for my work that lay ahead. This revelation also relieved me of some of the guilt I had been feeling in regards to the seemingly unfairness of life, where some, including myself, had plenty and others lived in abject poverty, although the purpose of that I still could not fathom.

Trust also came through as an essential component; believe and trust in what is happening and know that God will set in your path the people and circumstances required for you to fulfill your assignment, giving you the strength, the support and the energy you need to complete your work. Trust also that others are on their path as you are on yours and even though another's path may seem quite different, know and trust that your paths have crossed for a reason.

I found that with this attitude of trust and confidence in God and the journey, I no longer feared what the future might bring. I continued to feel an overwhelming sense of gratitude for what was unfolding and the events of my life, which had moved me from a place of desolation to one of joy, excitement and meaning.

CHAPTER XII

Opening the Door to Spirit

IS THERE ANYTHING you can do to encourage your own awakening? Can we hasten the delivery of the assignment, the knowing of our life purpose? I don't think so. People must do their own work if they are to fly.

This point has been graphically illustrated in the story of the crippling of a butterfly caused by the efforts of a kindly man, who, in attempting to relieve the butterfly of its hardship, pain and suffering, intervened by snipping open its cocoon. This actually ended up harming it, leaving it unable to fly, and so it spent its entire life crawling helplessly along the ground. Apparently the butterfly needs the struggle and resultant physical pressure of its own escape from the cocoon in order to force body fluid into its wings, without which the wings do not develop. And so, through the man's seemingly helpful efforts to prevent pain and suffering, the butterfly was never actually able to take on its true role in life.

This seems to be a fairly accurate metaphor for the revelations which I was having, that my previous experiences, as difficult as they might have been, were necessary as prerequisite grooming for my assignment and my spiritual awakening. This process was confirmed by several others; that the assignment and spiritual awakening seems to come out of a period of adversity and that when a person is at their weakest, Spirit is likely to intervene.

What is the reason, than, for the telling of my story if not to enlighten others or to reduce pain and suffering?

One reason is to provide camaraderie and support for others having similar experiences, to validate their journey when others may be disputing what is happening or when self-doubt creeps in. I found Spirit guides all about, without whose support I may well have floundered on my mission. Affirmations came in various forms including through people, through books and poems, songs on the radio and from the natural world around me. I encourage you to look for your guides everywhere, even in your dreams! Be alert and mindful of the support you may be receiving—perhaps this book will be one of them—bringing the spark you need to light your inner flame.

Another reason for sharing the truths revealed to me is so that others can use them to strengthen their own resolve and commitment, and to gain hope and courage through difficult times, encouragement to keep the faith in hopes of a better tomorrow; and remembering those words to which I clung so fiercely in my worst of times—"Faith make things possible—not easy."

These truths and messages may also be helpful to those already on the enlightened path, giving a framework for thinking things through, inspiring further thought and bringing new insights. The sharing of these types of stories may also lighten the load of responsibility. I felt quite overwhelmed at times, feeling that the weight of the entire enlightenment of humanity rested upon my shoulders. Thankfully, the story of the butterfly came to my rescue!

Additionally my testament, the journey of my healing and of how I found meaning in life, may offer a different perspective for those seeking to understand the human journey, including our connection with Spirit, the role of Spirit in our lives and in our relationship with the world around us, both in its seen and unseen form.

And lastly, but possibly foremost, is to give the gift of 'Hope', hope for those going through seemingly hopeless situations, this hopeful story adding to their realm of possibilities. The final entry in my voice recording reflects on the role of hope in our lives and is offered to you here.

"What is Hope? Hope is a gift, hope is a state of mind, hope is a blessing, hope is energy, hope gives energy, hope extends optimism, hope is a giver of life and a giver of meaningful tomorrows!

"What can Hope do for you? Hope can give you comfort and can motivate you today, knowing that there can be a better tomorrow and that things can be different for you, for your friends, your family, and for the entire world.

"Where does Hope come from? Hope can be inspired by those around you, through stories such as this one, by those who believe in you, by Spirit and even out of blind faith; faith in yourself, faith in others, faith in the future and in humanity!

"Hope is something that everyone can have, rich or poor, people of all races, backgrounds and positions in life; hope is universal."

You only need to accept the gift.

EPILOGUE

HAVING COMPLETED THIS segment of my journey, where to next? Now, having been filled with a sense of hope and adventure, and buoyed up with a zest for life, a new chapter was to begin. The next movement of Spirit in my life was revealed to me through the life story of another, one who came to me from the distant past, one who told his tale of his search for meaning and truth but of whom I knew nothing at the time.

I found a book on a discount shelf in a bookstore titled *Siddhartha* (or rather as I've come to say — the book found me). As I was reading the story, I repeatedly said to myself, "this is me, this is how I feel." The Buddha had struck! This book — which gave the accounting of the Buddha's life — clarified my feelings and my desire to shed my old way of life. I realized that even though I lived in comfort and in secure circumstances, this no longer satisfied my soul.

But it was another little book — one which I found in the management section of a bookstore — that really pushed me over the edge. The book is called *Who Moved My Cheese* by Spencer Johnson, M.D. Within the covers of this book is a parable about four mice that, due to different attitudes and approaches toward handling changes, had remarkably different results when faced with the same set of circumstances. The "cheese" represents what one wants out of life. After reading this short but profound tale, I sat in my house, looked at my surroundings, and said to myself "there's no cheese left here!"

At the same time as these realizations were being thrust upon me, I was feeling a destiny call to the east, both symbolically as representing new beginnings and directionally as a career opportunity was materializing for me in the eastern area of our province; one where I would be in a position of leadership. And so, having faith in the process that was unfolding, I decided I would answer the call when it came. In anticipation of things to come, I readied myself; prepared myself professionally, gave away my superfluous possessions and sold my house.

Spirit did not disappoint me as some six months later I received that call, successfully applied for the position and moved into a new period of my life; surrounded by new people, a new community and a new landscape.

I hope you will join me upon the release of my next book as Spirit continues to intervene, providing me with new lessons and truths, and sets me firmly on this new path of faith and hope and purpose in life.

Love to all,
Sue

Listing of poems in order of actual occurrence: Page

ADDITIONAL THOUGHTS

Things Happen For a Reason

MY VIEW OF the life journey changed dramatically during those first few weeks of my spiritual awakening. I now believed that the pain and suffering of my past had served as a vehicle for this awakening and my current state of joy. My life was now filled with meaning and purpose, a new beginning revealed at every turn, with every interaction providing an opportunity for new discoveries, new lessons and new adventures. For this I openly showed my gratitude.

At the time, I did not question these feelings; however some with whom I shared my story seemed shocked by the thankfulness I was holding for those painful experiences which even extended to those who had inflicted that pain. When I sensed that others might think me a little strange for having such feelings, I became more guarded about sharing that aspect, although I continued to feel gratitude for my life as it had unfolded, with all of its hurts, pains and losses. As a result of my own personal experience and from the stories told by others I have come to believe that things happen for a reason.

This term 'things happen for a reason' is often used to explain something which is unexplainable and which, at the time, does not make sense. This phrase seems to serve as a comfort during painful events and provides a shortcut rationale when our conscious mind fails to provide us with the answers.

In order to explore this idea further—that things happen for a reason—I offer you here various theories and ideas about the human journey, the soul, how and why we exist, our purpose, and where we are heading. All of my personal beliefs include the idea that a 'greater power' than myself is at the helm.

Theories about the human journey abound across various religious and non-religious belief systems. The ideas which I offer are those I now view as 'possibilities,' some of which I openly embrace and for which I have a deep conviction; and some others that I have recently begun exploring. I ask that you keep your mind open to the possibilities and allow these ideas to sink into your conscious and subconscious mind. These ideas may spark something that lies deeply hidden there. I encourage you to explore further that which resonates with you.

Existence of the Soul

Firstly, let's consider the existence of the soul as a driving force for my awakening. This is not a concept that many of us have given much attention to during our formative years, other than in the context of religion. For example, when we consider the *psyche* — we find it means "the human spirit or soul." When we look up the definition of *psychology*, which by its suffix would imply the study of the human spirit or soul, instead we find that it is "the scientific study of the human mind and mental states and of human and animal behaviour" (from the online *Encarta Dictionary*).

There is no reference in this definition to the study of or an accumulation of a body of knowledge about the spirit or soul. Nor did I find this to be true during my university and psychiatric nursing studies which included many courses under the heading of psychology. These topics included introductory, behavioural, abnormal, and social psychology. None of these spoke about the soul. That in itself should be of interest to all of us!

Gary Zukav, in his book *The Seat of the Soul*, puts forward his belief that humanity has not yet evolved to the point where we can recognize the soul. We are limited to knowledge that we can attain through the five senses — and because of this, psychology is currently the study of the personality. He further puts forward that "because of this [our inability to perceive beyond the five senses] psychology is not able to understand the dynamics that *underlie* the values and behaviours of the personality."

Could the pain and suffering we experience actually facilitate the evolution of the soul? Zukav suggests we are evolving into a multisensory being which "acquires its knowledge through its intuition, and, in processing that knowledge, aligns itself, step by step, with its soul." He further says, "Awareness first enters an unaware personality through crisis caused by a collapse of the five-sensory personality to deal with the situation." This may well explain what happened to me as I went through my marriage breakup, uncertainty as to my life path, and the meaning of my existence.

Why has humanity not given serious thought and scientific study to the nature and workings of the soul? Jane Roberts, in the book *Seth — The Magical Approach*, offers this explanation dictated by Seth, a highly evolved spirit entity: "Science delegates the world of nature as the realm of exterior natural events . . . telepathy and clairvoyance, for example, are a part of natural effects, but they belong to a nature so much more expansive than science's definitions that they have been made to appear as highly unnatural eccentricities of behaviour, rather than as a natural component of consciousness. It is also for that reason they seem to fall outside of the realm of the sane . . . They [telepathy and clairvoyance] do not appear very well under the auspices of the scientific method, because the scientific method is itself programmed to perceive only information that fits into its preconceived patterns." In other words, only that which can be measured by the five senses is valued by science.

Up until then, for the most part, I had relied on science and my internal basic truths to conduct my life. Now things had changed. There was no body of scientific knowledge that could shed light on what had happened to me. Having been groomed to consider only the results of science as a basis to acquire new truths, I was the ultimate skeptic. Who or what could I trust?

As I began looking for answers to my questions, relevant material actually found me. One of these books is titled *Soul Search — A Scientist Explores the Afterlife* by David Darling. Imagine my excitement in finding someone who I felt might provide me with a scientific point of view! In this book, David Darling explores the topic of life after death. I would suggest this as a great starting point for skeptics such as I was at that time. I found myself on an emotional rollercoaster as Darling presented extensive review of the research on the features associated with near death experiences. Although he found that most of the reported aspects of the experience could be logically dispelled based on brain activity research, one which he said could not be explained away is that "As the experience unfolds, the subjects, it seems, become more and more conscious of everything except themselves." He further states that "This is the core enigma of the NDE. Why should it be that as the brain dies, consciousness expands? And why should it be that as consciousness expands, self-consciousness disappears?" An online version of his book is available for free at: www.daviddarling.info/works/SoulSearch/SoulSearch_front_1.html

Another scientist and self-confessed atheist, Francis S. Collins, gave me further insights. Collins is an American physician-geneticist who led the Human Genome Project. The aim of the project—completed in 2003—was to map every human gene and to learn how these genes are expressed, how the DNA sequences of those genes stack up against comparable genes of other species, how they vary within our species and how DNA sequences translate into observable characteristics.

During the time he worked on that project he was led from atheism to spirituality and a belief in a 'Creator.' He documents this journey in his book *The Language of God: A Scientist Presents Evidence for Belief.* Collins reflects on the phenomenon which C.S. Lewis described as "an unsatisfied desire in itself more desirable than any other satisfaction," and his own personal experiences in which he describes similar feelings as "a poignant sense of longing " and suggests that this 'desire' or longing may serve as "a pointer toward something beyond us." In this book he reconciles the role of scientist with a belief in God.

Although neither of these books provided me with scientific evidence for the existence of the afterlife, neither did they refute it, and, since these two men were scientists, I felt reassured.

Soul — What Is It?

If we put forward the notion that the soul exists, then what is it? Where is it located in our body and where does it go after our death, if indeed it goes anywhere? And if it does exist what is its purpose?

Here I offer you some ideas and beliefs about the soul which I have encountered during my quest. I also offer my experiences and thoughts about them, although I have not as yet come to any definitive conclusions on this subject. As one of my friends says "my experience of the afterlife is limited as I am still alive on planet Earth."

The Encarta online dictionary defines 'soul' in a number of ways. I have summarized these as follows:

— In Christian Science, Soul is the name for God.
— Soul is the complex of human attributes that manifests as consciousness, thought, feeling, and will — and is regarded as distinct from the physical body.
— Soul is the spirit that survives death. In some religions the spiritual part of a human being is believed to continue to exist after the body dies. The soul is sometimes regarded as subject to future reward and punishment, and sometimes as able to take a form that allows it to remain on or return to earth.
— There are numerous references to the use of the word 'soul' as reflective of an individual's or group's feeling states, character, moral nature, or emotional depth and sensitivity, either in the person or something created by a person.
— Soul is also defined as 'essence,' the deepest and truest nature of someone — what gives somebody or something a distinctive character.

In considering this concept as I used the term in my story and in my poems, my best choice would be to call it an *essence*, the deepest and truest nature of me. Characteristics that I ascribe to it include my soul as being something innate within myself, something that can be affected by others' behaviour — either positively or negatively; something that can guide my decision-making on my life path as I work toward accomplishing my life work or 'assignment'; and as something that can grow, change and evolve over time. Here are those excerpts referencing the soul:

- a small crack in the window of my soul
- a path of healing for my wounded soul
- new frontiers of my heart and soul
- the thing that he stole from the depth of my soul
- the pain caused by others to our souls
- to push pain into your soul, squeezing out your goodness
- clear windows to my soul

- the mind weak and thus the body and soul also
- The messages I received revealed what is truly important on this search for meaning, to the discovery of one's purpose and to the fulfillment of the assignment. Factors which interfered with these goals were referred to as 'enemies of the soul.'
- This book about the Buddha's life clarified my feelings and my desire to shed my old way of life. I realized that even though I lived in comfort and secure circumstances this no longer satisfied my soul.

Now, in reviewing this list, it is apparent to me that I believe I have a soul or I suspect I would not have made reference to it so often! I suggest that if you look deeply inside of yourself, you too will find something at your core that you cannot explain, something that provides you with insights, ideas and a deep knowing and understanding when you allow these to surface into your conscious mind.

Location of the Soul

Where is the soul located in the physical body? This seems to have been a topic of interest throughout the ages. The ancient Egyptians believed it was in the heart. In 1515 Leonardo da Vinci was denounced as a sorcerer for attempting to find the soul by dissecting the brain, following the belief of the time that it existed in the centre of the head.

Some believers claim that the soul is a substantial entity. American doctor Duncan MacDougall performed experiments in 1907 to measure the change in weight of tuberculosis patients as they died. He found that the average loss of weight was 21 grams. Details of his experiment can be found at www.snopes.com; use the search words 'soul man.'

More recently there have been efforts to locate the soul using modern day technology such as PET and CAT scans.

Interestingly, during a meditation where I asked the question as to the soul's location in the body, an answer came to me that the soul is an energy encoded and stored in our cells at the DNA level.

Soul's Purpose

If we accept it as fact that we have a soul and that it is immortal, then what is its purpose?

In her book, *Journey of the Soul,* Dr. Brenda Davies, a psychiatrist and past life regression therapist, provides us with compelling circumstantial evidence to help us understand the nature and purpose of the soul. She bases her conclusions on channelled wisdom, reports from those who have had near-death experiences, those who have worked closely with people who are dying, the teachings of major religions, and from her own work in past life regression therapy. She concludes that the soul is encoded with the cosmic laws which set out the basics of expected human behaviour which is to be true, honourable and just. It also carries information within it which will help us to live our current life and discover our life purpose — as well as the history of all our past lives.

According to Gary Zukav, "your soul is that part of you that is immortal" and "when the energy of the soul is recognized, acknowledged, and valued, it begins to infuse the life of the personality and when the personality comes fully to serve the energy of its soul, that is authentic power." He further states "this is the goal of the evolutionary process in which we are involved and the reason for our being."

Zukav observed that some of the world's great thinkers and writers such as William James, Albert Einstein and Carl Jung, to name a few, were motivated by something more than what was possible using the scientific model. He concludes that they were in fact mystics, going well beyond the five sensory thinking mode in their writings and conclusions. He thinks they were responsible for the evolution not only of their particular areas of study, but also of those who read their works. He believes that this motivating force comes from some other place beyond the personality and is leading us to our next step on our evolutionary journey.

It seems to me that our soul holds this force, and that by aligning ourselves with our soul we can generate the authentic power required to propel us on a positive evolutionary path.

Where does the soul go after our death?
How does it affect our current life?

What about the ideas of past lives, reincarnation
and the concept of karma?

Edgar Cayce talked extensively on these topics. He believed souls were created in the image of God on the spirit plane, to be companions for God. Cayce claimed that there was a 'falling out' or 'rebellion' of souls on the spirit plane which led to our separation from God. This separation was of our own freewill, which we have always had and will continue to have. Since God's will and desire is to be in unity with all souls, we are given the opportunity to incarnate on this earth plane. This provides a school as such, giving us opportunities to gain a growing awareness of the consequences of our thoughts, choices, and actions.

Cayce suggests that lessons to be learned in each incarnated lifetime are carefully planned while the soul is on the spirit plane, based on our individual progress thus far and in consideration of the needs of other souls. Further, if we successfully learn our lessons, we will remember who we are and once again regain full attunement with God. As a result of this attunement we will reconnect with our divinity, and therefore no longer need to return to this earth plane, although, according to some sources, some souls still choose to do so in order to help the rest of humanity. (*The Edgar Cayce Primer: Discovering the Path to Self-Transformation* by Herbert B. Puryear, Ph.D., 1982)

That in itself leads to another question: if indeed we do return to this physical plane to engage in another lifetime, why do we not remember our past lives in our new chosen lifetime? It has been suggested that everyone on this planet has past-life memories locked away in the subconscious mind and that these memories are affecting us now. Some people do in fact remember their past lives.

In *You Were Born Again to Be Together*, Dick Sutphen states: "The chain of cause and effect would trace everything that has ever happened in the universe back to some original cause. When the effect is felt in man, the cause was set in motion in the mind. The effects you are feeling now, both positive and negative, are the results of causes from this lifetime or from previous lifetimes. The seeds you are sowing now will bring forth the effects yet to come in this lifetime or future lifetimes."

Past life regression therapy, whereby this subconscious knowledge is uncovered, has been found helpful by many in dealing with current life problems and issues.

Here we might add the laws of Karma to this discussion. Karma, as cited in Hindu and Buddhist philosophy, refers to the quality of somebody's current and future lives as determined by that person's behaviour in this and previous lives (paraphrased from the online *Encarta Dictionary*). I understand it as a sort of goal-directed process through which the decisions we make in this life determine the nature of our next life struggles. This ultimately leads to enlightenment and a higher vibration so that we might return to God. I have read that for this to happen the soul needs to experience all aspects of the human journey to rid ourselves of karmic debt. For example I may have chosen to be a victim, perpetrator, male, female, healer, have a short life or a life of illness *before* returning to the earthly plane.

This may not resonate well with some people since this perspective holds us responsible for our current situation. However, in my mind, it also provides us with opportunities to choose freely and learn from our circumstance to free us from our karmic debt load. Gary Zukav claims "The soul is not confined to time as we know it and the release of negative energy benefits not only the current incarnation but all others, past and future as well as other aspects of consciousness."

In *The World's Great Religions: Life Magazine — Volume I: Religions of the East* we learn that, "People cannot fly from the effects of their own prior deeds . . . . Their karma is the principal factor in determining their happiness or unhappiness in life . . . . People reap that at that age, whether infancy, youth or old age, at which they have sowed it in their previous birth . . . . People get in life what they are fated to get, and even a god cannot make it otherwise."

Several years ago I attended a retreat offered by James Finley. He puts forward the idea that "all human suffering stems from our separation from Spirit." It seems to me that the information presented here reinforces and gives credence to his supposition. James Finley is a former Trappist Monk who was mentored by Thomas Merton and who today offers workshops and retreats across North America on "The Contemplative Way." I can personally attest that at my own 'awakening' — during which I experienced intense feelings of connection with Spirit—joy and happiness permeated my entire being.

My Purpose

Even with all of these ideas and the wisdom of the sages, the entire purpose of my existence continues to elude me, but one purpose seems to be clear—and that is to document my journey for others to read. That starts with this book. I also know that I have been called to help with the dilemma that earth and humanity are presently facing, in particular that associated with climate change.

My journey of discovery has led me down many roads. I especially value the teachings of the indigenous peoples of the world. Unlike most Western religions, their teachings and beliefs uphold a deep connection with nature and the earth. The current earth changes and the predicament in which we find ourselves are well described in the indigenous prophecies.

One upcoming event which some say marks the long awaited unfolding of these prophecies is that associated with December 21st, 2012, the date at which the Mayan calendar ends. As I understand it, this doesn't mean the *end of the world*, just the end of one era and the beginning of another. The indigenous beliefs give me hope and courage in facing these current times as all include the concept of 'free will' in making choices. We have an opportunity to create our future and determine what happens here on earth. In other words, we can choose our evolutionary path.

For example, the Hopi, an indigenous people of northern Arizona, have carried with them a prophecy of these times for some 1,000 years which speaks of the current predicament in which we find ourselves, facing issues of environmental devastation, natural disasters, and economic upheaval. Along with the prophecies, the Hopi were given the responsibility of sharing this knowledge with the rest of the world. The Hopi elders have embraced this responsibility wholeheartedly. Their history, the prophecies and guidance for us is well documented in *The Hopi Survival Kit: The prophecies, instructions, and warnings revealed by the last elders* by Thomas E. Mails, 1997.

It has been extremely difficult for the Hopi to ensure this knowledge, based on their culture and spiritual wisdom, survived to current times.

Many gave up their traditional ways, succumbing to the lures put out by the white governance with promises of land grants and improvements in their financial circumstances. But there were those who held fast to their responsibility and their dedication to keeping the knowledge and the traditions alive. They faced severe adversity, including the incarceration of their men for refusing to allow their children to be sent to government boarding schools and for resisting farming according to the government's instruction.

After several attempts to share this knowledge with the world at the United Nations Assembly, they were finally successful in doing so on December 10, 1992 — albeit very briefly as they were only allocated 10 minutes! Since then, the Hopi have continued to lobby and share their message at the United Nations forums, most recently at the Geneva Convention in October, 2011.

Along with all other indigenous prophecies, the Hopi also tell of a time when there will be a joining of the four races for the betterment of the entire planet. In the Americas, a common prophecy is for the joining of the *Eagle* of the north and the *Condor* of the south, which reflects the union and rising up of the native people across the continent. Their teachings are prophesied to bring opportunities for healing, both of our relationships with each other and of the planet. The *Peace & Dignity Journeys*, to which I have recently been 'called,' embodies this prophecy. I suspect that this too is a part of my 'purpose.' More details of the Journey and the Prophecy can be found at www. peaceanddignityjourneys.com.

I have also recently been drawn to a program called "Agents of Conscious Evolution," and have taken the 'Agent' training. This project is the spirit-led creation of Barbara Marx Hubbard, a visionary with extraordinary insights into our current world crises. She sees these times as an opportunity for the birth of a new, conscious, co-creating humanity, whereby we can choose who and what we want to evolve into rather than stumbling forward by chance. This program advocates and supports bringing the spiritual attributes of peace, love and harmony into the decision-making processes in governance. She and many other visionary thinkers around the world are joining their collective energies to assist in igniting an evolutionary leap to the next level of human consciousness. (www.birth2012.com)

With this exposure and involvement, I'm filled with renewed hope, faith and optimism for our future as a human race and for planet earth.

Closing Comments

For me, the most interesting aspect of all of these theories and belief systems I have offered are their common elements — whether based on a spiritual or evolutionary premise. These are the capacity for free choice, the potential for good and evil — and 'wisdom' which seems to involve goodness, purity, integrity, caring and love for the natural world and the rest of humanity. I believe our choices will be easier and create a happier life if we align ourselves with our purpose. That begins with listening to our inner wisdom and our higher self, the one that reaches beyond this physical world.

So I leave you with these thoughts and offer you these words as you move along your life path: 'things happen for a reason'!

Love to all,
Sue

PS I welcome any comments or thoughts you may have.
My email contact is Sue@sueostapowich.org.
To check out what else I'm up to please visit me at my website www.sueostapowich.org.

—NOTES—

—NOTES—

—NOTES—

—NOTES—

CPSIA information can be obtained at www.ICGtesting.com
Printed in the USA
LVOW060215200912

299566LV00002B/2/P